Attila the Hun

A Captivating Guide to the Ruler of the Huns and His Invasions of the Roman Empire

Free Bonus from Captivating History (Available for a Limited time)

Hi History Lovers!

Now you have a chance to join our exclusive history list so you can get your first history ebook for free as well as discounts and a potential to get more history books for free! Simply visit the link below to join.

Captivatinghistory.com/ebook

Also, make sure to follow us on Facebook, Twitter and Youtube by searching for Captivating History.

Contents

Introduction

In the popular imagination, Attila the Hun is among the most barbaric leaders ever. His warriors have the reputation of being ruthless, cruel, and bloodthirsty, as the Huns are believed to have been savages lacking any semblance of civilized culture.

The Huns raped and pillaged with abandon whenever the opportunity arose, and their raids into lands poorly protected by military outposts in the crumbling Roman Empire became legendary. The Huns under the command of Attila are thought to have been largely responsible for the collapse of the Roman Empire and the commencement of the Dark Ages in Europe.

The reputation of Attila and his people, the Huns, is at odds with reality. But examining the few historical records of his character and deeds reveal quite a different story. It is true that he was a calculating leader who was skilled at unleashing his fierce fighters when necessary. It is also recorded in history that he was a continual thorn in the side of the Romans. However, placed in historical context, Attila acted in ways that were common among leaders, both Roman and barbarian, in the first half of the 5th century. What is extraordinary about him were his uncanny abilities in negotiations with superior powers, his capacity for matching and exceeding his enemies in duplicitous behavior, and his successes as a military tactician on the battlefield.

Chapter 1 – The Origins of Attila and the Huns

The world in which Attila was born into in the early 400s proved to be a determining factor in his triumphs in warfare and his prowess in managing the expanding influence of the Huns. The age was ripe for the rise of a brutal adversary to challenge the highly civilized Romans and the less civilized barbarian tribes.

Attila and his elder brother Bleda were the sons of Mundiuch. Mundiuch was the brother of the dual leaders of the Huns, Octar and Rua (also known as Rugila or Ruga). There is considerable debate among modern historians as to how Hun society was organized. It is unknown whether the leaders of the Huns, whom the Romans called their "kings," were hereditary monarchs or principal warriors who achieved dominance based on their power and influence. It is likely that authority was won by one's demonstration of skill in warfare and buying loyalty through the distribution of monetary rewards from the leader's treasury. The Hun leaders certainly maintained their dominance by brutally eradicating any who challenged them.

Attila and Bleda, as youths, were instructed in the art of war, which included lessons on horseback combat, archery, fighting with a sword, and the use of a lasso. Excellence in horsemanship was a necessity among the Huns. It was through this skill that they pursued their main two means of earning a living as nomadic herdsmen and as pillagers of neighboring people. Both could be pursued simultaneously with some male family members remaining on the plains while others went off to war.

As well as learning about the arts of horsemanship, archery, and swordsmanship, Bleda and Attila acquired knowledge of the deeds of their ancestors. As children, they were exposed to the legends and sagas of the Huns, as the stories of their wars and struggles for power were preserved in songs and poems that were transmitted orally. Remnants of them have been preserved in later medieval and renaissance compilations of ancient epics.

There is no record of whether the training of Attila and Bleda involved an education in more refined skills. Some have said that they learned to speak the language of the neighboring Goths and the Romans. The notion that the brothers acquired some knowledge of Latin stems from the fact that a high-ranking Roman soldier by the name of Flavius Aetius was present as a hostage in Uldin's and then Charaton's court between the years of 410 to about 425 CE.

The brothers, who were to become dual kings of the Huns, were born somewhere in the Great Hungarian Plain, most likely in a permanent village rather than an encampment of nomadic herdsmen. The settlement in which they were born was likely built around a very modest palace in which the higher-ranking Huns advised the dual monarchs. It was from this rudimentary complex of buildings that the most powerful of the Huns exerted control in a centralized sovereignty over a rural population of nomadic herdsmen. These nomads followed their herds of horses, sheep, and goats as they moved from exhausted grazing lands to greener pastures.

Although historians do know what kind of professions the Huns undertook, other things remain a mystery. For instance, what language the Huns spoke is completely unknown. As an oral culture, they left no written texts. What we do know about the Huns is through a smattering of writing by Greek and Latin authors whose reports are naturally colored by prejudice. An example of this is the account of Ammianus Marcellinus, who in the late 4th century wrote that the Huns "exceed any definition of savagery." He said that they were distinguished by "compact, sturdy limbs and thick necks" and that they were "so hideously ugly and distorted that they could be mistaken for two-legged beasts." Marcellinus went on to say that although the Huns looked like humans, they ate their food raw, wore clothes made from mouse pelts and goatskins, slept outside in the freezing cold, and were immune to hunger and thirst. For Marcellinus, a man who might have never even seen the Huns and just relied on secondhand knowledge, the Huns were everything that the Romans were not. As such, they were categorized as barbarians.

Because the historical record of the Huns is only fragmentary, scholars have turned to archaeological evidence to throw some light on the kind of culture in which Attila and Bleda grew to maturity. The yields of archaeological research, though, are almost as scant as the written texts. We do know from archaeology what the Huns did not have. They did not build permanent homes of stone. Hunnic towns, of which there may have been but a few, did not even have stone walls. There have been, to date, no archaeological finds that reveal even the outlines of the kind of wooden dwellings described by a writer who visited Attila's court in 449. Excavators in Hungary have unearthed various metal cauldrons and only about 200 burial sites. And the Hun burial mounds contain only a few objects that can inform us of Hunnic material culture. For instance, some of the skulls from these mounds show signs of artificial flattening; it appears that as infants, the Huns had their heads bound with flattening boards. This kind of cosmetic deformation is common among various other so-called "primitive" peoples around the world.

The most interesting archaeological finds include bone stiffeners used in the manufacture of composite reflex bows, a few primitive gold headpieces, and a few gold harness decorations for horses. Their jewelry, a rare find in Hunnic archaeological excavations, is decorated with simple geometric patterns. Whether these represent the work of Hunnic goldsmiths is debatable. It is likely that such durable and valuable items that may have been kept, rather than traded away, were not produced locally but were treasure looted from elsewhere.

The Hunnic culture still remains an enigma for historians and archaeologists. As such, its origins are a matter of conjecture. Some believe that the Huns moved into the Eurasian plain from northern China. From there, around the middle of the 4th century, they crossed the Volga River, forcing thousands of settled ethnic Goths to flee and seek refuge along the lower Danube River within the Roman Empire.

The extent of the plains of Hungary was less than the broad Eurasian Steppe, which is where the Huns migrated into Central Europe around the end of the 4th century. With less land available to them in Central Europe, the ethnic Huns expanded their economy to include trade with neighboring peoples. In order to acquire assets such as Roman currency, gold, and other valuables which were efficient commodities for trade, the Huns engaged in organized theft or pillage from neighboring tribes and the Romans. There is no evidence that this was a traditional means of income before the Huns arrived in Europe, however.

The migration of the Huns across the Volga into Central Europe might have been caused by climate change or by pressure from other westward migrating peoples leaving Asia. As they moved westward, the wandering Hunnic herdsmen, traveling in wagons with their scant material possessions, came into contact with other tribes already occupying grazing lands. These peoples were absorbed into the stronger Hunnic culture. However, they still retained some of their existing traditions. Thus, what became known as the Hunnic Empire, stretching from Caucasus Mountains, the mountains between the Black Sea and the Caspian Sea, to the heart of Central Europe, was a multi-cultural society. Centralized control over this ethnically diverse population, as some were pure herdsmen nomads and others combined pastoral economies with crop growing and organized trading, required political acumen coupled with force. The most skilled at both was Attila, the successor to a line of leaders who played less prominent roles in the history of Europe and Asia.

When the Huns settled in Central Europe, the Roman Empire was in the process of crumbling into disarray. The once mighty central authority of the Roman emperors that exerted power over Europe, Asia, and North Africa was quickly eroding. The Sasanian Persians in the east and the previously pacified barbarian tribes in the west either swept across the Roman frontiers or revolted, putting vast swathes of the empire under the suzerainty of, according to the Romans, "savages."

This weakening of Roman control was a result of bad leadership, corruption, mutiny, and assassinations, along with a declining economy, increased dependence on unreliable non-Roman soldiers, and the division of the empire into two independent empires in 395. The inevitable consequence of splitting the once mighty Roman Empire into the Eastern Roman Empire, also known as the Byzantine Empire, ruled from Constantinople, and the Western Roman Empire, ruled from Ravenna, was a continuous rivalry for dominance. The almost non-stop plotting by the Eastern and Western emperors as they strove for power furthered their inability to effectively deal with military crises internally and on the frontiers. There were more than enough of these calamities to challenge even the most skilled leaders. The tribes of barbarians that had previously been kept outside Rome's frontiers due to the greater power of Rome sensed a weakening of the borders, and attracted by Rome's wealth, they began to invade. Some of the barbarians' forays into Roman territories were brief. Others involved permanent settlements in territory forcibly taken from poorly led, badly trained, and underfunded Roman legions.

Chapter 2 – The Wars of the Huns Before Attila

When Byzantine Emperor Theodosius II sent his troops to Mesopotamia to attack the Persians in 422, the king of the Huns, Rua, with Octar's assent, took advantage of the situation by leading his warriors south from the Great Hungarian Plain. In dugout boats and rafts, Rua and his men crossed the Danube, the northern border of the Byzantine Empire, and pushed into Thrace, which would have included parts of modern-day Bulgaria, Greece, and European Turkey.

This incursion by the Huns was different from the Roman idea of territorial expansion as the Huns were not motivated by land acquisition. They did not attempt to create settlements or military encampments in conquered territories in order to exert permanent authority like the Romans. The sole goal of Hunnic warfare was to acquire wealth through pillage. As will become evident in the chronology of the Hunnic raids into both the Eastern and Western Roman Empires, economic success depended on pushing into new, potentially rich sources of income. Once the Huns had completed the despoliation of a particular territory, it was necessary to move on to greener pastures or wait for the Romans and their subject peoples to rebuild their settlements. For the Huns, their pillage economy was carried out much in the same way as their nomadic herding economy.

Theodosius, unfamiliar with the Hunnic custom of warfare, feared the loss of Byzantine control over land so close to his capital city, so he withdrew his troops from Mesopotamia and redeployed them in Thrace. After exhausting the resources for plunder, the Huns negotiated their own retreat from the territories within the Byzantine Empire. They agreed to leave the lands they had pillaged in return for an annual payment from the Byzantine emperor. Theodosius and Rua differed in how they defined these annual payments of 350 pounds of gold. The Huns considered the tribute to be a recognition of their superior power. The Byzantine emperor saw the annual financial settlements as a ransom for captive soldiers.

In 430, Octar, the other co-ruler of the Huns, led a pillaging expedition across the Rhine River into the Roman province of Gaul (modern-day France). He and his rapidly moving mounted warriors swept up treasure from the Burgundians, an East Germanic barbarian tribe that the Romans had reluctantly permitted to settle within the empire. It was, according to most of the later Roman and French writers of history, Octar's attacks that inspired the Burgundians to abandon paganism and convert to Christianity. As Christians, they entreated God for deliverance from the scourge of the Huns. Their conversion from their pagan ways was apparently rewarded. The Burgundian prayers were answered when Octar, after a night of gluttony, died of an explosion of his gut. The Huns, in the absence of a leader, were forced to withdraw, cross the Rhine, and return home with their booty.

It wasn't long before Rua, now the sole ruler of the Huns, repeated his bid for Byzantine gold. Theodosius sent his troops away again, this time to aid in a battle against an East Germanic barbarian tribe known as the Vandals, who were besieging the Western Romans in North Africa. Rua, who may have felt aggrieved at the Byzantine failure to render his tribute, broke the treaty of peace, seizing the opportunity in 434 to pillage the towns and farms in Thrace that had escaped his first incursion or had been restored in the brief period of peace. As well as treasure, he was also in search of refugees from subject tribes who had crossed the Danube and voluntarily joined the Byzantine army. He boldly moved east, threatening Constantinople itself. It was probably due to Rua's sudden death from unknown causes that the Huns stopped their advance before reaching their goal. No matter how attractive the opportunity to loot the wealthiest city in the world was, the Hunnic warriors were reluctant to continue without a strong commander.

The warriors' loyalty to a new leadership was probably established as they made their way back home north to the Great Hungarian Plain. Although there is no historical record, it is possible that among them were Attila and his brother Bleda. It is very likely that both polished off their training as warriors not only on Rua's two expeditions into Thrace but also with Rua's co-ruler Octar's incursion across the Rhine.

However, what is known is that with Rua dead on the verge of besieging Constantinople, Attila and Bleda, clearly capable of using brute force and clever arguments, established themselves as co-rulers of the Huns.

Chapter 3 – An Alliance Between the Huns and the Romans

There were very few Romans in either the Eastern or Western Roman Empires who had firsthand knowledge of the Hunnic culture. One who did have a good understanding of the Huns was a high-ranking military officer by the name of Flavius Aetius. He was born around 391 in modern-day Bulgaria, not far from the Hungarian home of the Huns. He rose in the ranks of the Roman army and reached the status where he could serve the Western Roman emperor as a suitable hostage to be held as surety for peace with opposing peoples. He was first placed into the hands of the Visigoths, the western branch of the Goths, as a guarantee against Roman reprisals against them. The peace guaranteed by Aetius as their hostage had followed the Visigothic rampage, led by their king Alaric, throughout the crumbling Roman Empire, first around Constantinople, then in Greece, and finally in Italy in 401. Alaric's attack on Milan in 402 forced the removal of the imperial court of the Western Roman Empire to evacuate and settle in Ravenna. Even though the Roman Senate paid Alaric off and delivered hostages to him, among whom was Aetius, the Visigoths continued their bellicose behavior, eventually sacking Rome in 410. This was purely a symbolic act as the once-great metropolis had fallen on hard times. The patricians, or ruling class, continually squabbled over the scant resources while the Senate was a hotbed of intrigue. The general population was dependent on handouts while the once magnificent metropolis fell into disrepair.

Aetius, who had been Alaric's hostage between 405 to 408, was transferred to the royal court of the Huns. He stayed there for most of the reign of Uldin and that of his successor, Charaton, the predecessor of the kings Rua and Octar. Aetius probably learned the Hunnic language, and he certainly became familiar with their pagan customs, acquired an understanding of their system of warfare, and may have come to know the young Attila and Bleda. It was about this time that the two youths were refining their skills with the bow and horsemanship. The bow might have held a special interest to Aetius. The wooden composite reflex bow with bone stiffeners was used to great effect by horsemen approaching an enemy. These weapons were also useful in a retreat as a horseman could twist around and loose off arrows at pursuing enemies. This bow was much more deadly than the longbows used by the Roman *sagittarii*, infantry or cavalry archers.

When Aetius returned to service in the Western Roman Empire, the dangerously ambitious general fell out of favor and was exiled from the court in Ravenna. His restoration to power came at the insistence of the Huns who, after the death of the Western Roman Emperor Honorius in 423, forced Galla Placidia to take him on as an advisor. Galla Placidia was the extraordinarily powerful half-sister of Honorius, both being the children of Byzantine Emperor Theodosius I. This was probably accomplished by Aetius telling her that if he was not promoted, the Huns would invade the imperial city. At the time, Galla Placidia was struggling to establish her role as regent of the Western Empire. She schemed and fought to establish her imperial authority until her young son Valentinian was old enough to rule. Aetius, through subterfuge, disposed of any opposition to his influence on Galla Placidia and demanded that she appoint him commander of all the Western Roman troops. She, however, rejected Aetius' bold demand. With the death of King Octar and the retreat of the Hunnic forces across the Rhine, it appeared to Galla Placidia that Aetius' threat held no power. Emboldened by Aetius' apparent weakness, she made Aetius' archenemy, Bonifacius, a co-commander of the Western Roman armies. Bonifacius and Aetius settled their quest for power on the battlefield in 432. Although Bonifacius' troops prevailed, Bonifacius soon after died of wounds he sustained in combat. Aetius escaped retribution, as he sailed across the Adriatic Sea and made his way to the court of Rua, now the sole ruler of the Huns. It is not known whether Attila and Bleda were privy to the negotiations between Rua and Aetius. As a part of their training in statecraft, they might have listened in while Aetius tried to convince Rua to come to his aid in the power struggle in Italy. According to some sources, he was somewhat successful in his dealings with the Huns and returned to Italy with a contingent of Huns in his retinue. Others, however, state that Aetius failed in his pleadings. Once he returned to Italy, he convinced Galla Placidia that the Huns would soon come to his aid. Although this was a false claim, the regent was in no position to risk her power, so she appointed Aetius as the supreme military commander of the Western Roman Empire in 433.

In his role of commander of all the Roman troops in the West, Aetius faced a daunting task. The Western Empire was in dire straits. The Visigothic kingdom, now firmly established in Toulouse, threatened expansion. In the north of France, the Bagaudae, an alliance of small landholders, were revolting, and to the east, along the west bank of the Rhine, the Burgundians threatened aggression. Aetius turned to the Huns for help in regaining firm control over Gaul. In 435, he bargained with the new kings Attila and Bleda, offering a deal in which the Huns would be unopposed by the Romans in crossing the upper Danube and entering the Roman provinces of Pannonia and

Valeria. In effect, the Huns were given free rein to pillage in a portion of the Western Roman Empire. In return, the Huns agreed to supply warriors to assist Aetius' Roman troops in attacking the enemies of Rome in the province of Gaul. What attracted Attila and Bleda to this offer was the chance to establish a firm border with the Western Roman Empire by destroying the intervening Burgundians, who could at any moment move east, cross the Rhine, and enter the Great Hungarian Plain. Attila, who would prove to be a brilliant strategic thinker, recognized that if the Huns could eradicate potential invaders across the Rhine in Gaul and across the upper Danube, he and his brother could deploy their warriors to the south where they could wage war with the goal of acquiring treasure in the fabulously wealthy capital of the Byzantine Empire, Constantinople.

The Huns succeeded in destroying the Burgundians. Perhaps driven by the remembrance of their own defeat under Octar, they slaughtered and pillaged with great effect. How many Hunnic warriors fought in this expedition is unknown; however, the number of Burgundians slaughtered in this ethnic cleansing may have been as high as 20,000. The Huns' Christian Roman allies were aghast at the extermination of their co-religionists. However, for the Romans, it was a small price to pay for the removal of an obstacle which allowed Aetius' Roman troops to push north with the Huns and subdue the insurgent Bagaudae. The allied Roman and Hunnic armies then moved south to deal with the Visigoths, who had departed from their base at Toulouse and laid siege to the Mediterranean port of Narbonne, which was saved by the Roman and Hunnic forces. The combined armies then laid siege to Toulouse itself. There was considerable consternation among the Christian Romans when the Huns, on the eve of going into battle, consulted their pagan gods through soothsayers. In a skirmish outside the walls of Toulouse, the Roman general leading the expeditionary force was captured and executed by the Visigoths. The siege came to a standstill. The Huns, whose motive for fighting alongside the Romans was simply the acquisition of wealth, were reluctant to engage in an extended siege which could be unprofitable. They withdrew and made their way back home.

It is likely that Attila and Bleda were present throughout this Hunnic venture in Gaul. Their successes in the battles alongside the Romans would have provided them with a deep understanding of Roman military tactics, siege machinery, and Roman goals in warfare, which were distinctly different from their own. Beyond exterminating the Burgundians and learning of Roman tactics, the Huns had little else to gain from the battles. What benefit they obtained in the incursion into Bagaudae lands in northern Gaul and forcing the Visigoths back into Toulouse was the opportunity to pillage the countryside they passed through. The Romans turned a blind eye to these activities as bands of Hunnic horsemen regularly peeled off from the main force in search of whatever they could get their hands on. It is likely that the Huns were accompanied by a train of wagons onto which they loaded stolen food, gold, gems, and Roman currency.

Chapter 4 – Attila Attacks the Byzantines

In 437, when the Burgundians and Bagaudae were pacified, the Western Roman emperor, Valentinian III, who had achieved the age of majority, traveled to Constantinople to marry Licinia Eudoxia, the daughter of the Byzantine emperor, Theodosius II. No doubt Attila and Bleda saw that this union could be used to their advantage as they had helped the Western emperor remove his enemies in Gaul. Attila and Bleda arranged a peace conference with the emissaries of Theodosius with both Hunnic kings attending in person.

The negotiations in 439 at Margum (forty miles from modern-day Belgrade) did not start well as the Huns refused to dismount to talk with Theodosius' delegation. This was a brilliant ploy to establish the priority of Hunnic customs over Roman ones. And it certainly gave Attila and Bleda the upper hand. It was agreed by the two parties that the Byzantine emperor would render up all refugees from Hunnic lands who were living south of the Danube. These refugees must have posed a particular danger to the leadership of Attila and Bleda. After the refugees were delivered to the Huns, there was an execution of two young boys, blood relatives of Attila and Bleda, which helped to further cement their rule.

Theodosius' emissaries further agreed not to ally themselves with any enemies of the Huns. The Treaty of Margus, signed in 435, regularized trade so that markets were permitted at designated towns along the Danube. Most importantly, the emperor of the Byzantine Empire agreed to pay an annual "tribute" or "service fee" of 700 pounds of gold. This was double the amount of the previously negotiated payments during the reign of Rua.

For Theodosius, the advantage of successful negotiations with the Huns was the potential for their lasting pacification. With the Huns being paid to stay in their own lands, the Eastern Roman emperor could significantly withdraw troops protecting the border along the Danube, allowing him to send troops off to the east and to North Africa.

Shortly after this peace negotiation was concluded, the Vandals captured Carthage in North Africa in 439. This loss of a major port in the Western Empire's breadbasket was catastrophic for both the Eastern and Western Roman Empires. It was believed that the Vandals would inevitably launch seaborne attacks around the Mediterranean, so the defenses of the ports in both the Eastern and Western Empires were improved. In Constantinople, the walls were repaired, and a fleet was assembled to transport troops to North Africa. As soon as they heard that the Byzantine fleet had left Constantinople, Attila and Bleda restarted their war against Byzantine strongholds. Even with the number of Hunnic warriors being depleted since the failed siege of Toulouse, the Huns attacked and captured the Byzantine trading port of Constantia on the north bank of the Danube in 440.

An emissary was sent from Constantinople to discuss terms with Attila and Bleda. The kings claimed that the existing peace treaty with the emperor of the Byzantine Empire was void. They complained that the bishop of Margum, the city where the peace pact had been agreed upon had led a raiding party to the north of the Danube. The Huns claimed that the bishop's followers had pillaged Hunnic graves and accused them of disturbing the burial sites of

Attila's and Bleda's own ancestors. The evidence for this allegation was probably fabricated by the Huns. Still, the kings demanded that the Byzantine imperial emissary hand over the bishop and any of his cohorts responsible for despoiling sacred pagan burial mounds. They also demanded, yet again, that the emperor turn over all the refugees who had fled across the Danube to escape Hunnic rule.

Attila and his brother eventually called off the peace negotiations and spent the next two summers pursuing their tried and true method of raiding cities, towns, and undefended farms south of the Danube. There is no historical record of this violence, but it takes little imagination to picture the devastation. The killing fields were doubtless littered with the bodies of innocent farmers and their families. Slaves and treasures were loaded on carts and taken north. In the case of the city of Margum, the populace debated whether to sue for peace and just hand over their bishop to the Huns. To save his life, the bishop took action. He fled north, crossed the Danube, and personally negotiated with Attila, offering to betray his townsfolk. On returning to Margum, the bishop convinced the Roman soldiers and his fellow citizens to attack Attila's troops when they were at their most vulnerable. They poured out of the city, intending to defeat the Huns just as they were disembarking from their boats crossing the Danube. Attila's troops, working in accordance with the bishop's subterfuge, had already landed on the south bank of the Danube and hidden in the undergrowth. They ambushed and destroyed the defenders of Margum, pillaging the city and gathering treasure wherever the opportunity presented itself.

Many of the Byzantine cities enjoyed what they considered adequate defenses. However, the Huns, from their observations in Gaul as allies of the Romans, had acquired a knowledge of Roman siege technology. Instead of riding around city walls and loosing arrows up at the defenders on the battlements, the Huns constructed a wheeled crane with a platform. From a vantage point above, the deadly archers would shoot down at the soldiers on the city walls. After having cleared a section of a wall, the Huns would bring in battering rams, patterned on those of the Romans. The rams used by the Huns in the siege of the city of Naissus (modern Niš in southern Serbia) are described in a historical document. They consisted of a suspended beam with a sharp metal point; this beam would be pulled back on short ropes then released to smash against the walls. Clearly, the Huns were not averse to adopting Roman technology when it suited their needs. When Naissus fell in 443, it was leveled by the Huns, and the citizens were either killed or captured. The captured were nearly as valuable as treasure, as they became a commodity of trade which the Huns could exchange for goods, primarily food.

With his army tied up in Sicily awaiting orders to embark for North Africa and attack the Vandals, Byzantine Emperor Theodosius II was hamstrung by lack of troops. It was only when peace was negotiated with the Vandals in 443 that he could order the return of his fleet. When the Byzantine army finally appeared to oppose Attila's and Bleda's warriors terrorizing the peoples south of the Danube, the shrewd co-regents led their mounted fighters back to the Hungarian plains.

The booty obtained by the Huns on their raiding expeditions and the Byzantine tribute payments were under the direct control of Attila and his elder brother Bleda. As co-regents, they distributed the treasure as they saw fit. Thus, both bought the loyalty of their subjects. Two years after returning home from their most profitable incursion into Byzantine territory, what may have been, up until then, a standoff between equals vying for power erupted into a violent fraternal dispute. In 445, Attila gained the upper hand, and Bleda was assassinated. However, there are no historical records describing the assassination. Long after, some believed that Bleda attempted to kill his brother, and the enraged Attila took up his sword and dispatched Bleda. It is unlikely that the end of Bleda did much to enhance the already powerful reputation of Attila as a bellicose and decisive leader.

The populace in the Western Roman Empire had already grown to be quite familiar with the kind of regime change undertaken by the

Huns. Constantine III, who was a self-declared emperor, and his son and co-emperor were executed by Constantius III in 411; Joannes, who had usurped the imperial throne, was defeated in battle and executed by Valentinian III in 425; Valentinian himself was assassinated in 455; and his successor, Petronius Maximus, was stoned to death by a Roman mob in the same year. The next four emperors of the Western Roman Empire were all killed by rivals.

Up until the removal of Bleda, it is not possible to attribute Hunnic victories and failures in war and in diplomacy to Attila himself. Either of the brothers could have been responsible for any of the events and victories in the history of the Huns. With Bleda removed from the scene, it is possible to get an understanding of the true character of Attila himself.

Chapter 5 – Attila Attacks the Byzantines Again

Attila, now the sole ruler of the Huns, recommenced the profitable Hunnic habit of pillaging Byzantine territories. He began by making a renewed demand for the return of refugees and the promised annual payment of tribute gold, since the Byzantine emperor had reneged, as was his habit, on meeting the terms of peace with the Huns in 443. Attila's demand was a strategic move because he was almost certainly aware that the Huns' ultimatum would be rejected. Emperor Theodosius, confident in the strength of his empire's defenses, refused, just as Attila expected. In early 447, at the head of his army, Attila crossed into northwestern Bulgaria. The first target of the Huns was the city of Ratiaria, as it was the headquarters of the fleet of Byzantine vessels used to patrol the Danube. This river port was leveled, and their ecclesiastical treasures were carted off with other loot.

Attila's aggression was met with by the Byzantine army that had marched up from Thrace. The Huns engaged with the well-organized imperial troops, under the command of General Arnegisclus, in a pitched battle on the River Vid in the town of Utus. Arnegisclus was motivated by revenge; he had led a contingent of forces when the Huns defeated the Byzantines in 443. But neither Arnegisclus nor his soldiers succeeded in their goal of routing the Huns. The general was actually killed. There are, as usual, few historical accounts of the battle, but some say that both sides suffered serious losses. Whatever the technical outcome of the battle was, whether it was a Byzantine or a Hun victory, Attila still commanded enough Hun horsemen to push farther into the Eastern Empire, even destroying the largest city in Thrace, Marcianopolis, in 447. This was a particularly galling setback for the Byzantine emperor as Marcianopolis was an important commercial hub and a center of the Christian faith in the region. It had once even served as the temporary capital of the Eastern Empire. Its destruction demonstrated yet again to the Byzantine emperor the power of the Huns. Theodosius, if not already convinced of the extreme danger of Hunnic attacks in Byzantine Balkan territories but the potential for a siege of Constantinople itself, set about redeploying his army and keeping his capital safe behind its walls.

An earthquake in 447 had partially ruined the integrity of Constantinople's massive defensive walls. Early in his reign, by 413, Emperor Theodosius II ordered the rapid reconstruction of the damaged walls of Constantinople. The project is said to have taken a mere sixty days. The fast-track wall-building may or may not have been a factor in Attila's decision to retreat and cross the Danube into Hungary with his fighting men and their substantial pillaged treasure. This was to be Attila's last raid on the now depleted resources of the Eastern Roman Empire. It was to the west that he now turned his attention.

Chapter 6 – Attila Foils a Byzantine Plot

In 449, Attila sent Edeco, one of his high-ranking warriors, to Constantinople. With him was a Roman, Orestes, who served Attila as a court secretary. He was particularly useful for his knowledge of Latin. When Edeco was ushered into the throne room of the imperial palace, it was without Orestes, who was commanded to stay in a waiting room. After prostrating himself before the emperor, the roughly dressed Edeco attempted to state Attila's case. First, a letter in Latin, probably composed by Orestes, was read to the emperor. In it, Attila, presenting himself as an equal to the emperor, said that even though he had sent four embassies to Constantinople, he was still awaiting the promised return of refugees. Further, the Byzantine forces had not withdrawn to the agreed upon border to the south of the demilitarized zone comprising the land between the Danube and a line five days' journey south. When Edeco attempted to expand on Attila's demands, the only member of the imperial court versed in Hunnic, a secretary named Vigilas, was called to translate. Edeco stated that if Attila's demands were disregarded, a renewal of war might occur.

Having stated Attila's case, Edeco and Vigilas were ushered to the apartment of the eunuch Chrysaphius, a high-ranking official in the imperial bureaucracy. It was in this less than formal environment where the detailed negotiations were to be carried out. Edeco, through Vigilas, complimented Chrysaphius in the usual diplomatic style, saying that he was impressed with the opulence of the imperial palace. Chrysaphius replied that Edeco could avail himself of Byzantine riches if he would act on the behalf of the emperor and betray his Hunnic master. Feigning friendship, Chrysaphius then enquired about the details of how the Hunnic court was organized, how Attila selected his closest advisors, and other intelligence that could assist the Byzantines in their negotiations or battles with Attila. The conversation ended with Edeco agreeing to Chrysaphius' proposal that he return to Attila's court, kill his master, and then return to Constantinople where he would be showered with wealth.

Edeco demanded fifty pounds of gold which he said was necessary to bribe Attila's bodyguards; however, it was also impossible for him to carry this gold with him as it would inevitably be discovered by some of Attila's men. It was agreed that Vigilas would travel with Edeco back to Hungary. When the right opportunity presented itself, Edeco would send a message through Vigilas that the gold should be sent. In order to maintain plausible deniability, it is assumed that Emperor Theodosius II distanced himself from the plot.

To augment the credibility of the Byzantine embassy to Attila, Maximinus, a soldier with an excellent reputation, was chosen to be Theodosius' ambassador. He was charged with taking a letter from the emperor to Attila. Maximinus, however, was not informed of Chrysaphius' and Edeco's plot. As a token of goodwill, Maximinus was to bring along what Theodosius claimed were the last seventeen refugees in his possession. Also in the embassy was a scholar of rhetoric named Priscus of Panium, who would later go on to write a history of Byzantium; it is one of the few historical texts documenting the deeds of Attila. In the entourage were also the translators Vigilas and Orestes and a Byzantine merchant, Rusticius, who was conversant in Hunnic.

Priscus reported one untoward event on the journey from Constantinople to Attila's court. Stopping for supper outside what remained of the town of Serdica (modern-day Sofia), recently laid to waste by the Huns, an argument broke out between Edeco and Vigilas. The conflict was over whether Attila could justly claim that his power came directly from the god of war as Edeco claimed. Vigilas defended his belief that the Byzantine emperor had a greater claim to power as his authority was given to him by Christ. The dispute was likely a ruse to direct attention away from the plot in which Vigilas and Edeco were key players.

After crossing the Danube, the first error in protocol occurred when the Byzantine ambassadorial party pitched their tents on a hill overlooking the encampment of Attila. According to the Huns, no foreigners could set themselves up above their leader's position; Edeco likely did not advise against this as his goal was to foment confusion in the negotiations. After the Byzantine encampment was relocated, Edeco and Orestes hastened to a meeting with Attila. It was in this meeting that Edeco revealed what had happened in Constantinople, including the details of Chrysaphius' plot. He also revealed the contents of Theodosius' letter to Attila that Maximinus had been ordered to deliver.

Maximinus, although innocent about knowing the plot, did not get along well with the Huns in the beginning. Scottas, one of Attila's closest advisors, arrived in the Byzantine camp and demanded to know what Maximinus had to offer. Maximinus, standing on the protocol of Byzantine diplomacy, claimed that he would not divulge the contents of his message from Theodosius to a third party. Scottas departed but soon returned and recited the entire contents of Theodosius' letter, saying that if Attila already knew all the Byzantine ambassador had to offer, the party should depart immediately.

However, Maximinus adamantly refused to abandon his mission, and Priscus, saving the day, convinced Scottas to intercede with Attila through flattery. The Byzantine emissaries were then invited to meet with Attila. Priscus, who might have been expecting to meet an extremely ugly barbarian, was disabused of his prejudice. He described Attila as short and broad-chested with a large head, small eyes, a flat nose, dark skin, and a partially gray beard. During the audience, Attila lashed out at Vigilas when he said that there were no more refugees in the Eastern Empire. In a rage, Attila said that if it were not for the rules of diplomacy, he would impale the cheeky man and leave his body to be consumed by birds. Attila ordered Vigilas to hurry back to Constantinople in the company of a Hunnic ambassador and return with all the refugees in Theodosius' hands. While he was away, Maximinus was ordered to stay where he was and not use the gold in his possession for any purpose other than buying food. Edeco pulled Vigilas aside and told him that their plot was on schedule and that Vigilas should bring the gold required to bribe Attila's bodyguard.

Following the inconclusive negotiations at Attila's encampment, Priscus and Maximinus were taken to Attila's principal residence in northwestern Hungary. Attila's permanent home impressed Priscus, who admired the large wooden palace complex that was situated within a wooden wall equipped with towers. The Byzantine emissaries were also shown a smaller palace, the home of Onegesius, Attila's principal advisor and brother to Scottas. Soon Attila arrived in the town, and a crowd of women lined the road. The procession ended with the women singing joyful songs and Onegesius' wife welcoming Attila with a ritual platter of food that symbolized the family's loyalty and subservience to their king.

Again, Priscus smooth-talked several influential Huns, even inveigling an invitation to the home of Erecan, one of Attila's favorite wives. When he met her, she was reclining on a richly upholstered couch, supervising a number of women as they embroidered pieces of linen with colorful beads. (Archaeologists have actually unearthed quantities of glass beads and ones made from amber and coral in regions once occupied by the Huns.) Priscus and Erecan exchanged gifts, and among Priscus' offerings may have been elaborately decorated Byzantine gold jewelry.

Maximinus was eventually granted an audience with Attila. Priscus reported that the Byzantine envoy was subjected to a more or less, take-it-or-leave-it ultimatum by Attila, as Maximinus was told that the Byzantine emperor should accede to Attila's stipulations for peace or there would be war. Even though the negotiations ended on a sour note, Attila proffered a dinner invitation to Maximinus. Upon entering Attila's palace, Priscus and Maximinus saw Attila seated in the middle of the hall. His advisors and his sons sat on one side and the high-ranking Huns on the other. After a round of the Hunnic version of toasts, tables were brought in and set with silver plates and gold goblets. When night fell and the candles were lit, Priscus reported that the jewels worn by all the guests shimmered in the flickering light. The after-dinner entertainment was especially noted by Priscus. It consisted of bards singing songs about Hunnic victories in war, who were followed by a madman who entertained the Huns with his insane rantings. The Huns apparently found this most amusing. What stood out for Priscus at the banquet was Attila's behavior. He was dressed in simple clothes, drank from a wooden cup, and ate sparingly. The only time Attila exhibited any emotion was when he warmly embraced his youngest son, Ernak.

Maximinus, annoyed by being seated far away from Attila and Onegesius, was unable to exchange words with the people he had come to talk to. He, as a Byzantine envoy, was unprepared to be treated in such a shabby way, and he departed before the conclusion of the feast.

At a second banquet, Maximinus was seated closer to Attila. He was subjected to a rant concerning one of Attila's secretaries, a man named Constantius. It was explained that Constantius had been sent to Attila by the Western Roman commander Aetius and that Constantius had lived with the Huns and served Attila loyally. Attila said that Constantius, on a mission to Constantinople, had been promised a bride by Theodosius, but the marriage did not occur as Constantius' fiancé was claimed by the powerful Byzantine general Flavius Zeno. Attila told Maximinus that Theodosius must straighten out this situation and deliver the bride to Constantius forthwith. If, said Attila, taunting the Byzantine ambassador, Theodosius was unable to control his officials, then Attila was willing to help him exert authority.

Maximinus and Priscus broke camp and set out for Constantinople. Along the way, they encountered Vigilas and his son who were on their way north with the gold promised by Chrysaphius to finance Edeco's plot to assassinate Attila. When Vigilas arrived at the town where Attila had his palace, he was arrested and the fifty pounds of gold confiscated. Vigilas was interrogated by Attila himself who demanded the truth or else he would kill Vigilas' son. After revealing the plot that Attila was already familiar with, he was imprisoned. Attila then sent off Vigilas' son to Constantinople where he was to demand a further fifty pounds of gold from Chrysaphius as a ransom for his father.

Attila also sent the Latin-speaking Orestes to confront Emperor Theodosius II with Chrysaphius' treachery. He ordered that his emissary wear one of the bags used to hold the gold confiscated from Vigilas so that Theodosius would immediately understand the failure of the plot. The confrontation between Orestes and Theodosius led to no admission of guilt by anyone in the Byzantine court. Most were convinced by Chrysaphius' outright denial that there was no assassination plot at all, and Theodosius solved the problem by paying for a cover-up. He sent a delegation to Attila with, as it is recorded, enough gifts to buy off the aggrieved king. Enough gold must have been proffered to have Vigilas released, and Constantius was also promised a wife of equal status and wealth to the first one he had been promised. Attila, after demanding that the tribute payments continue, agreed to release Byzantine captives, drop his demand for the return of refugees, and clarify prior agreements by stating that the Huns had no claim to any territory south of the Danube. Chrysaphius' plot was never mentioned again, and Vigilas, as a failed plotter, kept away from Constantinople until Theodosius died of injuries sustained in a hunting accident in July of 450.

Theodosius' successor, Marcian, quickly purged the Byzantine bureaucracy, killing the powerful palace eunuchs, Chrysaphius being among them. It was when Vigilas returned to Constantinople from his self-imposed exile that he was interviewed by Priscus. It became clear to the history writer that Attila had known of the treachery of the Byzantines in his meeting with Edeco and had cleverly strung the plotters along so that he could gain the most advantage from the exposure of their plan.

Chapter 7 – Attila's Diplomatic Strategy Evolves in the West

In the spring of 450, the eunuch Hyacinthus appeared at Attila's court. Hyacinthus, who had traveled from the Western Roman capital of Ravenna, announced that he was an envoy not from Emperor Valentinian III but from his sister, Justa Grata Honoria.

Honoria, ever since reaching the age of twelve when she became available for marriage, had been virtually imprisoned in Ravenna. Having inherited her mother's, Galla Placidia, independence of mind, she railed at being held as a marriage pawn to be used by Valentinian as he saw fit. She, it is said, smuggled lovers into her apartment and was impregnated by one of them. Her mother and Valentinian sent her off to Constantinople where it was intended she be reformed by austere female relatives imbued with the Holy Spirit. The instruction in good Christian behavior, which included submission to male authority figures, seemed to have fallen on deaf ears. Upon returning to Ravenna, Honoria promptly fell out of favor with her mother, who had become a Christian ascetic, someone who renounces material possessions and physical pleasures in order to reflect on spiritual matters. Honoria also continued her habit of acting independently.

Valentinian promised Honoria to an Italian aristocrat in a brazen attempt to solidify his own power as emperor. There was, in Valentinian's mind, a grave danger in having an ambitious sibling like Honoria available for a union with someone who was also ambitious and from the imperial bloodline.

Honoria, now in her thirties and bridling at her renewed confinement in the Imperial Palace in Ravenna, refused to cooperate with her brother's plans. Secretly, she sent an emissary, Hyacinthus, to ask for the help of Attila in dealing with her brother. The emissary proffered a payment in gold and promised Attila that should Honoria prevail in her goal of obtaining an imperial spouse, more gold would follow. In order to prove the validity of Hyacinthus' offer, he presented Honoria's signet ring to Attila.

Attila certainly would have known all of this about Honoria. In all his decisions with respect to negotiating with the superior powers in both the Eastern and Western Empires, Attila relied on a constant flow of information. His clever manipulation of opponents in peace councils and his brilliant decisions on when and where to lead his warriors on pillaging expeditions suggest that he was skilled in sorting out unreliable gossip from accurate reconnaissance. So, Attila understood that he could only gain an advantage by using any and all of those involved in opposing Valentinian. He grasped the opening offered by Honoria and sent Hyacinthus back to Ravenna with the message that he would help the emperor's sister out of her matrimonial predicament by marrying her himself.

When he got wind of Honoria's duplicity, Valentinian had Hyacinthus tortured. The unfortunate eunuch revealed everything about his discussions with Attila. Furious, Valentinian attempted to send Honoria off to the husband chosen for her, but she adamantly refused to budge from Ravenna. Galla Placidia intervened in the conflict between her two offspring, and Honoria was allowed to remain in Ravenna.

Attila was informed of Galla Placidia's intervention in the domestic dispute in Ravenna. He was most certainly dismissive of Valentinian's plans for Honoria, and he would have found Galla Placidia's meddling in the affairs of her daughter to be unwarranted. Honoria was to be his wife as she had indicated by giving him her signet ring. In the fall of 450, he sent a delegation to Ravenna to announce his engagement to Honoria. Attila's emissaries also demanded that Honoria be granted the title of joint ruler of the Western Roman Empire. This attempt by Attila to promote himself by marriage from King of the Huns to Emperor of Western Rome was indeed a bold move and guaranteed to raise the ire of everyone at the court in Ravenna.

There can be little doubt that Attila knew that his demands would not be met by Valentinian. The emperor simply responded by stating that Honoria was already promised to another man and that a woman could not rule the Roman Empire, so even if Attila managed to take her as a bride, he would not be emperor.

At about the same time as Attila's emissaries were making his demand for the hand of Honoria in Ravenna, he sent a delegation to Constantinople where they were to negotiate with the new emperor, Marcian. They demanded the arrears in tribute the Huns had negotiated with Theodosius. The Roman officials said that they would not pay "tribute" but would, if Attila maintained peace, give the Huns "gifts." The importance of this semantic distinction was fully understood by Attila. He knew perfectly well in advance that his insistence on "tribute" would be rejected as had his proposal to Honoria in the Western court. His sending of ambassadors to the Western and Eastern emperors was intended to create a pretext for waging war on both.

Attila, by nature a talented strategic thinker, would never consider simultaneously opening two fronts of battle. However, it is a sign of his skills in statecraft that he put it in the minds of both emperors that he might. In the words of Jordanes, a great 6th-century Byzantine historian, "Beneath his great savagery, Attila was a subtle man and fought with diplomacy before he went to war."

Chapter 8 – Attila Raids Gaul

Aetius, the commander of the Western Empire's army, attempted to convince Valentinian that the best way to deal with a potential Hunnic attack was to maintain a strong Roman military presence in Gaul. He believed that if the Huns crossed the Rhine, they would ravage a great deal of the province of Gaul. And if Attila attacked the Visigoths headquartered in Toulouse, the results could be devastating to Roman interests as well. If the Visigoths defeated the Huns or vice versa, they would be emboldened by their victory and expand their ambitions for conquest, thus requiring a concerted effort by the Romans to contain them.

Hearing the news that the Huns were already moving beyond the Rhine, Valentinian, with his back against the wall, agreed with Aetius that the Romans should enlist the Visigoths' assistance in fighting the Huns. This represented a major change in the Romans' dealings with the Visigothic kingdom. The agreement to become allies involved Valentinian conceding to the Visigothic king, Theodoric, legal authority over a significant portion of Roman Gaul, but it was a pragmatic solution to the problem of the Huns. It also headed off Aetius who Valentinian knew to be a constant schemer intent on overthrowing him.

Attila was well aware of the difficulties facing Valentinian, so he took his raiders north where they first demolished Metz, which was some 150 kilometers (a little over 93 miles) from the Rhine frontier. From there, the Huns have been said to have moved against Reims. According to a medieval legend, when the Hun horsemen reached the cathedral at Reims, they were met by Bishop Nicasius. They decapitated him as he was reciting a psalm seeking deliverance from the Hun scourge. The last few words of the psalm were apparently issued from his severed head as it lay at the feet of the Huns' horses. This so terrified the Huns, said later biographers of St. Nicasius, that they galloped from the city leaving it intact. Something similar may have happened at the city of Troyes, south of Reims. There, Bishop Lupus, according to later legends of the saint, marched out to confront Attila. He asked the Hunnic leader who he was, and Attila is said to have responded, "I am Attila, the whip of God." That this happened is unlikely, if not impossible, for Attila never converted to Christianity. It is related in the biography of St. Lupus, the savior of Troyes, that it was due to him that a miracle occurred. When the gates of the city were opened to the Huns, they were struck by a blinding light from heaven and passed in one gate and out the other without harming any of the residents. In the later Middle Ages and the Renaissance, the motif of Attila acting as the "whip of God" to punish the sinful inhabitants of Christian cities proliferated in ecclesiastical literature.

The truth of what happened during the early days of Attila's incursion into northern Gaul is likely more prosaic and not the stuff of legends. Attila financed his expeditionary forces through the distribution of loot. Unlike Roman soldiers who were paid a fixed amount of cash for their services, the income of Hunnic warriors depended entirely on what they could steal and cart off. Success in theft depended on the efficiency and number of wagons to transport loot. During an expedition where the pickings were good, the transport of booty might become difficult. It is likely that this was what happened during Attila's first days across the Rhine. What should also be remembered is that Attila's war had a distant goal: the acquisition of Honoria as his bride. Ravenna was a long way off from northern France, though, and this explains why the Huns did not bother attacking well-defended cities like Reims and Troyes. It was a simple calculation of the risks of delay caused by laying siege to cities which may or may not have fallen to the Huns.

It is unknown whether Attila laid siege to the city of Orléans as he moved south. He most likely did not. Legend has it that the bishop of Orléans himself went to seek the aid of Aetius and the Visigoths at the town of Arles over 300 miles to the south. He, so the story goes, convinced the Romans and the Goths to come to the rescue of his hometown. Upon returning home, he convinced the faithful to pray to God for deliverance. The invocation of the divine worked. Just as the Huns had begun to use their battering ram against the city walls, deliverance arrived in the form of the Roman army and allied Visigoth fighters.

However, the Byzantine historian named Jordanes, writing around 551, described the event of the previous century in different terms. He wrote that prior to the appearance of Attila at Orléans, the Romans and Visigoths had constructed a system of ditches and earth mounds along the route leading to the city. Attila, wrote the historian, was discouraged by this impediment and was also apprehensive as to whether his fighters would last in any protracted battle. The invading Huns turned east with the Romans and Visigoths hot on their heels.

At the end of June 451, the two sides faced off. The Roman and Visigoth armies were bolstered by Burgundian and Bagaudae fighters. These two groups overcame their dislike of Aetius who had, in 437, permitted his allies, the Huns, to ravage their towns and countryside. They were motivated by a stronger hatred of the Huns themselves who had been merciless in their slaughter.

The Huns were not without allies, though. They were joined by Ostrogothic warriors, members from the eastern branch of the Goths, drawn from clans north and south of the Danube. Some of their leaders enjoyed particularly cordial relations with Attila who no doubt gave them generous gifts, the rewards of joining the Huns on looting expeditions.

The two armies met on the Catalaunian Plains, located somewhere in modern-day Champagne, in June of 451. A description of the battle was recorded by Jordanes. At first, the Romans captured an incline where they could shoot their arrows and propel spears down on the Huns and their allies. The uphill attack of the Huns was repulsed, and the combined Roman and Visigoth armies drove them from the slope. Jordanes then says Attila gave a long speech to inspire his fighters. This is standard fare in historical writing at the time, as Attila is unlikely to have taken the time to deliver a lengthy harangue in the midst of battle.

Whatever happened, the ensuing bloody battle was indecisive. Theodoric, King of the Visigoths, fell on the battlefield along with countless warriors on both sides. By dawn the following day, the Huns had circled their wagons and were ensconced behind this protective barricade. Jordanes wrote that Attila, in the midst of his soldiers, vowed to fight to the death. The following day, Attila learned that the Visigoth allies of the Romans had decamped and were headed south. He knew this could very well be a ploy to draw the Huns out into the open, so he ordered his warriors to stay hidden behind the wagons. It was only when he was told that the Roman soldiers were also leaving the battlefield that he ordered horses to be hitched to the wagons and rode off to the Rhine with his mounted troops, and their Ostrogothic allies went off with their cargo of treasure.

There is no consensus among modern historians as to why the Romans and Visigoths marched away from the Catalaunian Plains. King Theodoric had been accompanied in the campaign by his son Thorismund, and the son seems to have exhibited considerable strategic skill in the actual battle. However, he may have been somewhat of a naïve politician, and it is said that Aetius convinced him to return to Toulouse immediately to claim the throne of his deceased father. The conjecture among some historians is that Aetius acted extremely duplicitous at this point in time. On the day after the battle, when the Huns could have easily been surrounded and defeated, some believe that Aetius secretly visited Attila, told him that Visigothic reinforcements were about to arrive, and that for a hefty bribe, he would convince Thorismund to go home. According to this tale, told by Fredegar, a 7th-century Burgundian chronicler, Aetius then went to the camp of the Visigoths, convinced Thorismund that Hunnic reinforcements were coming, and that if Thorismund handed over a generous settlement, he would convince Attila to retreat across the Rhine. This story sounds rather unlikely, but with duplicity being rampant in the era of the decline of both the Eastern and Western Roman Empires, it could be true. It is certain that Thorismund was rightly worried about his succession to his father's throne. However, two years after the Battle of the Catalaunian Plains, he was assassinated in Toulouse by two of his brothers, one of which was to succeed him as Theodoric II.

Because the descriptions of the events on the Catalaunian Plains are of a later date and thus became infected with myth and legend, they cannot be relied on as accurate. This has led historians to engage in guesswork. One hypothesis is that Aetius wanted the Visigoths to leave the area and refrain from decimating the Huns. It is surmised that by engineering a standoff on the Catalaunian Plains, Aetius could have had a long-range plan. Often, the total annihilation of the army of an adversary is not the wisest move. The complete removal of the Huns would certainly mean that the Visigoths would expand their control over Roman Gaul. Without the continued threat of Hunnic raids, without Attila always on the horizon, the Visigoths could concentrate on fighting the Romans and almost certainly solicit the help of the Burgundians and Bagaudae as well. Similarly, Aetius maintained power by having a well-oiled fighting machine available to fight against or fight with the Huns as circumstances demanded.

Just as modern historians hypothesize on the various strategies of the Romans, Visigoths, and various other ethnic groups within the orbit of the Western Roman Empire, so also would have Attila. There is more than enough evidence to suggest that he was not an unthinking barbarian. He was an astute leader with a deep understanding of the motives of his allies and adversaries. He outsmarted them on several occasions, combining force and diplomacy. The strange circumstances surrounding the Battle of the Catalaunian Plains are understandable if they are attributed to Attila himself. He may have thought that by circling his wagons and holding out, he would give the fragile Roman coalition time to disintegrate. He also likely understood that the death of King Theodoric would throw the Visigoths into confusion. Without their leader, he could expect their tenuous alliance with their traditional Roman enemies to become frayed. And, in fact, it did. Aetius, with the absence of the Visigoths, could not successfully surround the Huns with his depleted troops. Attila's advantage was that his wagons held not just treasure but also foodstuffs looted from farms. He, his men, and their hardy horses could have endured a siege of some length.

With the departure of the Visigoths and then the Romans, the Huns escaped complete destruction. Attila and his men did not have to fight to the death. If the story of Aetius' complex strategy after the Battle of the Catalaunian Plains is true, he made a strategic mistake in letting the Huns escape. Attila, never one to be at a loss in finding new sources for pillage, was about to engage in one more violent incursion into the Western Roman Empire.

Chapter 9 – Attila Raids Italy

The emperor of the Byzantine Empire, Marcian, grasped the opportunity to take advantage of Attila's expedition in Gaul. While Attila was distracted, Marcian cut off all payments of gold to the Huns. Shortly after the Hunnic leader returned home with his troops, Marcian sent a representative to Attila, and the talks did not go well. Attila's first demand was that the tribute payments be reinstated. As a demonstration of his power, Attila humiliated Marcian's ambassador by stripping him of all the gifts he brought and then threatened to kill him if he did not render up the tribute gold. The emissary scuttled back to Constantinople, leaving the question of tribute gold unresolved.

Both the Eastern and Western Roman Emperors believed that Attila, smarting from his defeat on the Catalaunian Plains, presented no threat. They should have instead questioned Attila's tactics, which according to Jordanes were, "shrewd and cunning. He threatened in one direction and moved his troops in another."

In the summer of 452, instead of crossing the Rhine into Gaul or heading south across the Danube into Byzantine territory, Attila launched a lightning strike southwest across Slovenia and into Italy.

The bold move was based on Attila's thorough understanding of Emperor Valentinian's military dilemma over this. Valentinian certainly didn't want to seek the aid of the Visigoths, as inviting them into Italy to fight the Huns was extremely dangerous. If the Huns were driven off by the new King of the Goths, Thorismund, he would be likely to turn on the imperial court in Ravenna. It was up in the air whether Thorismund would, if asked, even come to the emperor's aid. He had troublesome, ambitious brothers in Toulouse who he could not leave alone as they would plot his overthrow. Valentinian also had the option to call back Aetius to defend Italy. It was questionable whether the general would comply with an imperial order, and if he were to abandon Gaul, the Visigoths would have no check on their territorial ambitions. In the end, Aetius provided a limited number of troops for the defense of Italy.

Attila weighed the risks of his incursion into Italy and concluded that swift strikes along the head of the Adriatic Sea would open the way for his approach to Ravenna and his ultimate goal, capturing Honoria, his rightful bride. The plan was interrupted when Attila decided to lay siege to the wealthy trading port of Aquileia, which he succeeded in spectacularly. After breaching the walls, the Huns burned the city to the ground and massacred its inhabitants, making it impossible for the opposition to regroup and rise up against them. According to legend, the few Aquileians who escaped with their lives migrated along the coast and founded what was to become the city of Venice.

Moving on, Attila and his horsemen devastated the town of Pavia and then Milan, where the Western Roman Empire had once been centered. The former capital was rich with treasure, which the Huns, as was their habit, packed up to be hauled home. Emperor Valentinian, perhaps attempting to repeat a tried and true Roman tactic of scorched earth, left Ravenna and settled in Rome. With the crops burned in his wake, he hoped to discourage Attila from following him south. By the late summer of 452, Attila had set up camp in Mantua, 470 kilometers (292 miles) north of Rome. It was there that he received an embassy sent by Valentinian, which was led by Pope Leo I. Although there is no contemporary historical record of the encounter between Leo I and Attila, the event became standard fare in the mythos of Italy. (The event was even the subject of a painting by Raphael completed by 1514 in one of his frescos in the Apostolic Palace in the Vatican.) Legend has it that with the help of God and the spirit of Saint Peter, Leo I convinced Attila to remove himself and his soldiers from Italy.

It is unclear why Attila retreated without his promised wife. It may have been because the food supply for his men and horses was running out. Northern Italy at the time was suffering a drought, and the crop yields were low. It is additionally possible that an outbreak of malaria in the region reduced the efficiency of his army. More likely, he opted to retreat because their carts were packed to the brim with treasure already taken from the wealthy cities of northern Italy.

Chapter 10 – The Disintegration of Attila's Kingdom

While Attila was off ransacking northern Italy, the Byzantine emperor launched a series of attacks against the Huns in their lands north of the Danube. It may have been when he heard of Marcian's aggressive move that Attila decided the prudent course of action was to return to the Great Hungarian Plain and engage in war yet again with the pesky Byzantine emperor.

Upon reaching home, one of Attila's first acts was to send a mission to Constantinople. He threatened to wreak havoc in the Byzantine provinces because the tribute he was owed remained unpaid and promised that he would be crueler than ever with his enemies. It was, in his mind, not an idle threat, as he had followed up on all his previous ultimatums to the Byzantines.

In early 453, Attila married Ildico, who was said to be a rare beauty among the Huns. What number this wife was is unknown, though. Attila celebrated his nuptials well into the night, drinking and eating with his closest advisors and friends. The following morning, it was found that the door to the bridal chamber was battered down and Attila was dead in bed with Ildico wailing over his body. It seems that he suffered an aneurysm in his nose and in a drunken stupor choked to death on the blood. Of course, rumors that Ildico had killed him were rife.

When his officials informed Marcian of Attila's death, he said that he already knew of the king's passing, claiming that an angel had appeared to him in his sleep. The angel showed him a broken bow, which Marcian recognized as a symbol that his archenemy was deceased. For the Byzantine emperor and for Emperor Valentinian in Ravenna, the end of Attila confirmed that God had heard their prayers to be rid of this thorn in their sides at last.

Attila's Hunnic Empire was held together by the sheer force of his personality. The respect and obedience of his subjects, both Huns and non-Huns, were earned by his brilliance in leading successful raids into lands rich in treasure, and his manipulation of adversaries through diplomatic maneuvers was unparalleled at the time. Unfortunately, as was common with other barbarian regimes, his successors, lacking his leadership skills, squabbled and fought, and in doing so, they destroyed the once powerful central authority of the Hunnic people.

Three of Attila's sons, Ellac, Dengizich, and Ernak, managed in quick order to split the once unified Hunnic warriors into three factions. The ensuing chaos was seized upon by non-Hunnic peoples who were formerly loyal to Attila. In Slovenia, a coalition of clans revolted, and what remained of the Hunnic army was defeated by these insurgents at the Battle of Nedao in 454. Ellac was killed, and his warriors were decimated. The two surviving sons of Attila rode at the head of a contingent of horsemen and attacked the Ostrogoths along the Danube, but the Huns were again defeated in the Battle of Bassianae.

The collapse of the central power in the Hungarian plains precipitated the migration of peoples who were once content to submit to Attila's leadership. With the loss of regular income provided by pillaging expeditions, they sought other means of making a living. They moved south into Bulgaria, formally submitted to the authority of the Byzantine emperor, and settled on productive farmland. Later, they were joined by a huge number of Ostrogoths who moved in from the north and west. As many as 50,000 migrants settled in Thrace, many of whom would serve in the Byzantine army.

Attila's surviving sons, Dengizich and Ernak, tried to mimic their father's strategic diplomacy but failed miserably. Their threatening demand for tribute was dismissed out of hand. Dengizich, doing what his father had always done when opposed by an emperor, crossed the Danube with the intention of acquiring wealth and teaching the Byzantines a lesson. However, in 469, the Byzantine army easily defeated his warriors and killed him.

In the Western Roman Empire, things deteriorated rapidly after the death of Attila. The supreme military commander Aetius, who had matched Attila in political, diplomatic, and military skills, had been murdered in 454 by an enraged Valentinian III. By cutting down his principal means of executing power, Valentinian set in motion the death rattle of the Western Roman Empire. In 455, Valentinian himself was assassinated by Aetius loyalists. Later in the same year, the Vandals from North Africa sacked Rome and captured Valentinian's widow, Empress Licinia Eudoxia, and her daughters. The Vandals made off with a substantial amount of Rome's treasures, many slaves, and the last members of the Roman imperial family.

The consequences of the death of Attila had been predicted by his ally and adversary, Aetius, who believed that without Attila, the Western Roman Empire would disintegrate into chaos.

Conclusion

What Aetius could never have predicted was Attila's incredible life after death. He became the subject of myths and legends that continue to color our view of Attila even to the present day.

Attila is said to have referred to himself as the "Descendant of the Great Nimrod, King of the Huns, the Goths, the Danes, and the Medes." (This is, of course, the stuff of legend. That Attila would be able to trace his ancestry back to a biblical king who built the Tower of Babel defies reason.) His power was recognized by the 6th-century Byzantine historian Jordanes, who wrote that Attila wielded the "Holy War Sword of the Scythians" given to him by Mars and was thus "prince of the entire world." What was believed to be this sword was held up in the royal court of Hungary in the 12th century as a symbol of a royal lineage leading back to Attila. The surname of Attila was also once popular in Hungary, but its use has declined in recent years.

Tales of Atli (Old Norse for Attila) were integrated into orally transmitted sagas recorded in texts dating from the 13th century. In the saga *Atlakviða* (*The Lay of Atli or Attila*), Gunnar, King of the Burgundians, and his brother Högni are lured to Attila's court by the offer of valuable gifts. The brothers already have great wealth, but they are tempted by Attila's offer. By subterfuge, the Huns try to find out where the Burgundians have buried their gold. However, they do not reveal it, and both Gunnar and Högni are barbarously murdered by Attila's men. Guðrun, their sister and Attila's wife, prepares a banquet for Attila, and when he is well into the meal, she announces that they are eating the flesh of their two sons. Guðrun later kills Attila in his bed and burns down Attila's palace and all the buildings in its compound. *Atlakviða* exists in a written form dating from 1270, but as an orally transmitted story, it may date from three centuries earlier. The story is a good one, and like most of the legends about Attila, it has the requisite drama of murder and cannibalism.

A similar story is told in the *Saga of the Völsungs*. In this epic tale, Guðrun has a dream interpreted by Brynhild, which foretells her marrying Attila, that her brothers will be killed, and that she will kill Attila. The stories in this saga were adapted by Richard Wagner for his opera *Der Ring des Nibelungen* (first performed in 1876) and used by J.R.R. Tolkien in his story *The Legend of Sigurd and Gudrun* (dating from the 1930s). In Tolkien's novel, Atli (Attila) marries Gudrun, and Atli in his lust for gold kills Gudrun's brothers. In retaliation, she kills her two sons and makes goblets from their skulls. After drinking poison from one of the skull cups, Atli collapses on his bed. Gudrun rushes in, stabs him, and burns the palace and the surrounding town.

In 1812, Ludwig van Beethoven conceived the idea of writing an opera about Attila but never completed it. However, Giuseppe Verdi did produce an opera, *Attila*, in 1846. The libretto was based on the play *Attila, King of the Huns* by the German writer Zacharias Werner (1768-1823). The story is an imaginative narrative of Attila's expedition to lay waste to Italy.

At the dawn of the 20th century, Attila and his Hunnic warriors acquired especially insidious reputations that were an exaggeration of historical reality. In 1900, the German Kaiser, Emperor Wilhelm

II, gave a speech in which he lauded Attila and the Huns' military skills. He then urged his German fighting men to emulate Attila and the Huns, who they knew from old legends popularized by Richard Wagner in his operas.

While Kaiser Wilhelm's words may have worked well to raise morale among the German military, they also were used to inspire, through fear, Germany's adversaries in the two world wars. The strength of anti-German sentiment that evolved on both sides of the Atlantic in the first half of the 20th century ensured the widespread use of the epithet "Hun" among soldiers fighting Wilhelm's and Hitler's armies, as the nickname for the Germans emphasized what one could expect of them on the battlefield. This explains, in part, the popular notion today that Attila was one of the vilest leaders in history and that his Hunnic warriors were bloodthirsty brigands.

Attila's bloodthirsty status in the modern world partly stems from the prejudice he faces in sources written by Roman and Greek authors. Although he and his warriors were indeed violent, this was fairly commonplace in the era in which they lived. However, Attila was more than that. His looming, vicious reputation in history overshadows his brilliance and his clever strategies in contending with greater powers for the purpose of gaining wealth for himself and his people.

Here's another book by Captivating History you might be interested in

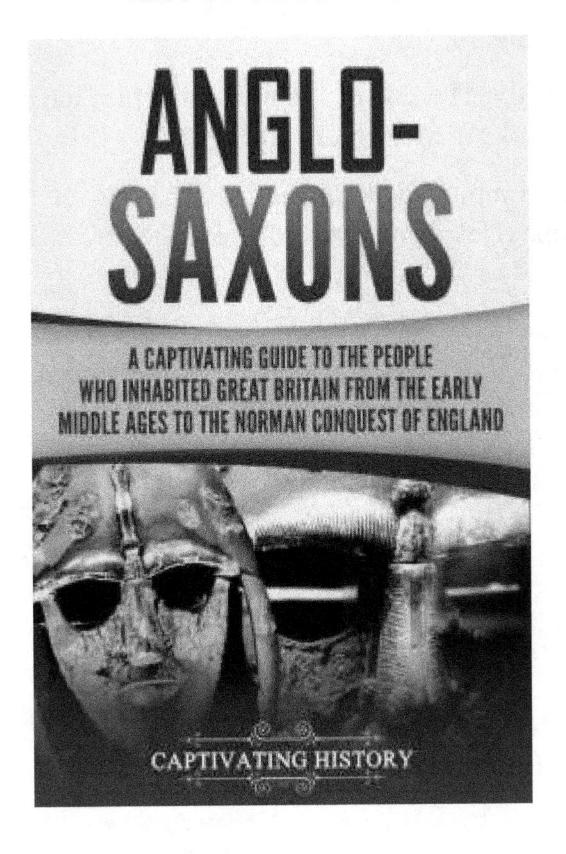

Further Reading

Christopher Kelly, The End of Empire: Attila the Hun and the Fall of Rome (New York: W.W. Norton, 2009).

P. J. Heather, Empires and Barbarians: The Fall of Rome and the Birth of Europe (New York: Oxford University Press, 2010).

Printed in the USA
CPSIA information can be obtained
at www.ICGtesting.com
LVHW010148060923
757372LV00005B/55